Emotional Intelligence

Control Your Emotions and Eliminate Fear (Build Self Confidence, Boost Your Social Likability, Improve Interpersonal Connections, IQ, EQ)

Lance P. Richards

Emotional Intelligence: Control Your Emotions and Eliminate Fear (Build Self Confidence, Boost Your Social Likability, Improve Interpersonal Connections, IQ, EQ)

This book was self-published with the amazing help of Self-Publishing Made Easy Now! [1] . You can grab a free copy of the checklist that started my journey here: FREE Self-Publishing Checklist [2] .

[1] https://selfpublishingmadeeasynow.com/xpjv

[2] https://selfpublishingmadeeasynow.com/free_checklist

Table of Contents

1 - Introduction

I want to thank you and congratulate you for downloading the book Emotional Intelligence – Control Your Emotions and Eliminate Fear! By reading this book, you have taken the first step in learning to control your emotions and your life. Your journey toward building a stronger Emotional Intelligence and reaping the benefits of a healthier, fuller life starts now!

This book contains proven steps and strategies on how to become a truly empowered individual. Discovering the role that your emotions play in your life story will enable you to implement strategies to guide yourself to future success. Controlling your emotions and eliminating fear is all about taking the reins! This book will help you to identify negative emotions and learn to conquer them.

Here's an inescapable fact: you will need an understanding of Emotional Intelligence to make positive changes in your life. Emotions are powerful and complex. Research shows that Emotional Intelligence is everywhere.

If you struggle with social interaction, anxiety, stress, or even anger, you may need to take steps to improve your

Emotional Intelligence. This book will help you to understand what Emotional Intelligence is, why it is important, and how you can use it to reach your goals.

Emotional Intelligence is both a gift and ability. Many lucky individuals are born with a naturally high Emotional Intelligence. We see many of these individuals in politics, the entertainment industry, and in leading positions in today's corporate business.

If you do not further develop your Emotional Intelligence, your entire life will be affected. Developing your Emotional Intelligence will give you powerful tools to navigate your professional, social, and private life. A high Emotional Intelligence strongly contributes to a happy, successful life story.

It's time for you to become an amazing individual! This book will help you to build your self-confidence, boost your social likeability, and improve your interpersonal connections.

We will explore the relationship between IQ (intelligence quotient) and EQ (emotional quotient) and how these factors influence your life. We will provide proven strategies to boosting your Emotional Intelligence, and provide your next steps in this journey. Congratulations, and good luck!

2 - What Is Emotional Intelligence?

Emotional Intelligence is a popular term in the media today: but what is it, exactly? This is a question Psychology researchers have been exploring for many years. Leading experts in Psychology and Neuroscience will confirm that there are many "types" of intelligence. You may have heard some individuals identify themselves as "book smart" or "street smart" or "money smart."

In simple terms, you can think of those with a high Emotional Intelligence as being "emotionally smart." Like any form of intelligence, some fortunate individuals are naturally gifted with high intelligence in some (or all) areas. The good news is that Emotional Intelligence is a type of intelligence that you can train!

With a little discipline and commitment, even those with a very low Emotional Intelligence can master the skills needed to become savvy, high-Emotional Intelligence individuals. Building your Emotional Intelligence can lead to the following practical benefits:

- Learning to recognize important emotional cues in

others

- Learning to identify and respond appropriately to the triggers that trip your own negative patterns

- Learning to replace negative emotional patterns with positive ones

- Using your skills to navigate a social world

Emotional Intelligence is the unseen conductor that guides human interaction and society. Research has shown that those with a high Emotional Intelligence have gone on to reach success in both their private and professional lives. Those with a high Emotional Intelligence claim greater life satisfaction and stability than those of their peers.

High Emotional Intelligence individuals can include CEOs, Professors, Politicians, Gurus, and other public leaders. Research has shown a link between Emotional Intelligence and overall Intelligence (IQ): building a higher Emotional Intelligence will boost your IQ and lead to a happier, more successful life.

"Chapter 2: What is Emotional Intelligence" will begin by giving you the tools to understanding Emotional Intelligence and its role in your life. In this chapter, we will cover the two parts of Emotional Intelligence and important terms for understanding Emotional Intelligence.

Once we build your knowledge on what Emotional Intelligence actually is, we will proceed to Chapter 3, in which you will learn how Emotional Intelligence influences your life.

Later, we will help you to identify the emotional patterns in your life that you want to change and give you proven strategies for taking control. You will find practical advice for managing a variety of situations. Remember, every individual is different: use this book as a journey into yourself!

What are the two parts of Emotional Intelligence?

Emotional Intelligence is an elusive topic. Defining Emotional Intelligence is difficult because the subject is very broad. A quick internet search will have you confused and bewildered: there are too many opinions and ideas to gain a solid concept of Emotional Intelligence!

Luckily, scientists have been working on the question with peer-reviewed, trustworthy research. Professional investigation into emotional intelligence has narrowed down the subject into two specific parts:

"Trait" Emotional Intelligence

"Trait" Emotional Intelligence refers to the specific traits that contribute to your Emotional Intelligence. In thinking about Trait Emotional Intelligence, your personality and "born-with" traits come into play:

- Are you an introvert or an extrovert?

- Are you an optimist or a pessimist?

- Do you persevere or do you "give up"?

- Are you independent or codependent?

These aspects of your personality contribute to the ways in which you process and express emotions, which is an important part of your overall Emotional Intelligence.

Determining which personality traits contribute to your Emotional Intelligence is a complex process. Research shows that humans cannot be easily divided into groups or types: for example, you cannot definitively sort every individual into the labels of "introvert" and "extrovert." Humans fall along a continuum, with some being more extroverted or more introverted than others.

Your personality is formed by a combination of genetics and experiences. That is, researchers are unable to determine what parts of your personality were inherited, and which parts you learned through social interaction. This means that your behavior may change depending on the situation.

Some individuals may be introverted in the classroom, but come alive during a Friday night party. Others may be loud and outgoing in academic settings, but quiet and closed off in large social groups.

It is important to understand that your emotional reactions do not exist in a vacuum: the larger environment is always at play. Consider the following example:

A wife returns home from a bad day at work to find her husband with another woman. She is shocked and angry. She reacts by hitting this woman, breaking her nose. The woman is taken to the Emergency Room and presses charges against the wife for assault. The wife is arrested.

The wife in this situation lost control of her emotions and reacted in a way that was ultimately destructive to herself. When considering this situation, ask yourself:

- Did she lose control because of a personality trait,

like a bad temper?

- Was her control weakened by a bad day at work?

- Was she reacting to an intolerable situation?

- Did she naturally have an underdeveloped Emotional Intelligence?

The truth is, her response to the situation was probably influenced by all of these factors! Your Emotional Intelligence takes contributions from your genes, your life, and your current environment.

Researchers provide Trait Emotional Intelligence as a definition of Emotional Intelligence that is influenced by your genes and the environment in which you grew up and surround yourself with. Trait Emotional Intelligence is a combination of the following factors:

Temperament

Research shows that those with a more optimistic temperament are more likely to perceive events as positive, leading to a more appropriate and controlled emotional response.

Controlling Moods

Those with a high Emotional Intelligence are able to recognize and manage their moods with more skill than those with a lower Emotional Intelligence. Individuals with mood disorders especially have difficulty with identifying moods, regulating moods, and maintaining a positive outlook.

Interpretation and Coping Skills

Your personality is influenced by the way you interpret your environment. Those with an extroverted personality are more likely to interpret "bad luck" as a challenge, and cope more effectively. Effective coping skills lead to the cultivation of more positive emotions.

The personality traits most commonly linked with the influence of Emotional Intelligence are extroversion, introversion, and "neuroticism." Neuroticism is a term used by Psychologists to describe those who consistently exist in a negative mood state.

Those with neurosis are often anxious, frustrated, angry, sad, or depressed. Unsurprisingly, neurotic and introverted individuals seem to have the most difficult time measuring and regulating their mood, while extroverts seem to easily maintain a positive mood state.

Remember that Trait Emotional Intelligence is only one part of our quest to define Emotional Intelligence. As researchers and statisticians love to say, "correlation is not causation!"

This means that although a high Emotional Intelligence is correlated with those that are extroverted, it is still possible for an introvert to build and maintain a strong Emotional Intelligence. Understanding all sides of Emotional Intelligence is only the beginning!

"Ability" Emotional Intelligence

A second definition for Emotional Intelligence is known as "Ability" Emotional Intelligence. This is a new approach to the study of intelligence that proposes Emotional Intelligence as an additional form of intelligence.

As we discussed at the beginning of the chapter, there are many different "types" of intelligence. Researchers have formally identified Emotional Intelligence as a "type" of intelligence by defining "ability" Emotional Intelligence.

Researchers provide Ability Emotional Intelligence as a

definition of Emotional Intelligence that is formed by your capacity for managing your emotions.

Research into general intelligence has shown that individuals have different "capacities" for critical thinking, verbal reasoning, spatial reasoning, quantitative reasoning, etc. Maintaining a high Emotional Intelligence may be representative of a higher capacity for managing emotions: thus, "Ability" Emotional Intelligence.

It is important to recognize that Ability Emotional Intelligence refers to a cognitive ability. This is different from the definition of Trait Emotional Intelligence in that an ability is not governed by your personality.

There are plenty of extroverts and introverts who show similar abilities in areas like math, science, and literature. Recognizing that Emotional Intelligence is, in part, an ability means that you can build your capacity for Emotional Intelligence: it is not simply something you are born with or born without.

The Emotional Quotient

Research shows that Emotional Intelligence is measurable separately from general intelligence. Your general intelligence, or IQ, is a crude, general measure for clinically defined intelligence. The researchers that put forth the definition of Emotional Intelligence as an ability argue that Emotional Intelligence is a measurable cognitive ability.

Some are born with natural talent (Trait Emotional Intelligence), but everyone has to build and hone their Emotional Intelligence. The research argues that there is a Quotient, similar to the "Intelligence Quotient" (IQ) to measure Emotional Intelligence. They are calling this the "Emotional Quotient", or EQ.

Research has found that EQ has a close correlation with IQ: the higher your EQ, the higher your IQ tends to be. Your EQ is determined by how you perform on "Emotional Quotient" tests, just as an IQ is measured by your performance in "Intelligence Quotient" tests.

A low IQ measure is not always indicative of a low overall intelligence: thus, a low EQ measure is not always indicative of a low Emotional Intelligence. This means that EQ and Emotional Intelligence are not the same thing: the Emotional Quotient is a number that measures your Emotional Intelligence.

As you continue reading, remember that your Emotional Intelligence is affected by a variety of factors. When seeking to improve your own Emotional Intelligence, take time to reflect on your own life—your genetics, your life history, and your current situation—and consider how these factors may influence your Emotional Intelligence today.

3 - Emotional Intelligence in Your Daily Life

Now that you are well-versed in the two definitions of Emotional Intelligence, we can begin to explore the role that Emotional Intelligence plays in your daily life. Emotional Intelligence appears in the ways that you react to situations and the ways in which you interact with others.

Processing and managing your emotions has an effect on you and on the larger society around you. This means that Emotional Intelligence is at play everywhere, but particularly in your education, your career, your marriage, your social relationships, and even in the way that you handle emergencies.

Emotional Intelligence can be overwhelming, and it raises many questions. Some common questions include:

- If Emotional Intelligence is everywhere, how do I identify it?

- How do I know if I have a low Emotional Intelligence?

- How does Emotional Intelligence show up in my life?

Let's go through some specific situations and see if you can spot individuals who are acting with a high Emotional Intelligence, and individuals who are not. We will offer an explanation at the end for each scenario. We will offer examples of Emotional Intelligence in school, marriage, social interactions, and in dealing with fear.

Emotional Intelligence in School and Studies

Situation 1

Rachel is a college student. She has had a difficult semester: her boyfriend dumped her, she's living far from home, and she doesn't make much money at her job. Finals are approaching. Rachel is stressed, exhausted, and anxious. She can't sleep. The night before her big finals, Rachel goes out and parties with her roommate. The next day she is hungover and oversleeps. She fails the semester.

Situation 2

Stephanie is also a college student. It is her senior year! Her semester has been difficult: she had to take some extra classes to fulfill enough credits to graduate. Finals are approaching, and she wants to get to graduation! Her parents got divorced this semester and can't help her pay for bills.

She has been working many overtime hours to pay for a post-graduation vacation, but because of the divorce, she had to put that money into school. She is exhausted and stressed out about finals.

As finals week approaches, Stephanie knows that she is going to need time to study and to unwind, so she takes a week off of work. She takes time to calm down every night before bed so she can get a good night's sleep. She aces her finals and holds her head high at graduation!

Analysis

Which of these students displayed a developed Emotional Intelligence in making decisions? Rachel has had some hard luck: but instead of managing her bad moods and finding constructive ways to deal with her anxiety, she chose to use alcohol to calm down, and failed everything. By not managing her stress and frustration, she reacted in a very destructive way!

In contrast, Stephanie took steps to manage her stress, kept herself calm, and aced her tests. She recognized the emotions she was feeling and took the time to address them.

Stephanie showed the traits of a person with a developed Emotional Intelligence, and this helped her to succeed in school.

Emotional Intelligence in Relationships and Marriage

Situation 1

Chris lives with his wife. He has been very caught up in work lately and hasn't been cleaning up around the house. His wife has been searching for a job and has been spending a lot of time at home. She has been doing all of the cleaning, as Chris has been too busy.

Chris has been very excited about his advancements at work and doesn't notice that his wife has been very quiet. He is surprised when, one night, his wife gets very angry at him, shouting that he never helps her with cleaning. Chris is unsure what he did wrong.

Situation 2

Andrew lives with his husband. He has recently been promoted at work, forcing him and his husband to move across the country. Andrew is used to moving and loves the new location, but his husband has never left home before and is homesick. Andrew's new position is taking off, but his husband is struggling to adapt and hasn't found a great job.

Andrew notices how frustrated his husband has been, and plans a special date for them to be together and talk it out. His husband admits his frustration, and he and Andrew come up with a plan to make things better. Both Andrew and his husband are satisfied that the new location is going to work out.

Analysis

Relationships are more complex for our emotions than handling personal challenges like studying for college finals. This is because there are now two individuals who need to act with Emotional Intelligence to make their situation work. Emotional Intelligence is not only about managing your own emotions: it is also about being in tune with the emotions of others, especially those closest to you.

In the first relationship situation, Chris seems to be an extrovert with a high ability for managing his own emotions. He is positive and excited and isn't experiencing any negative emotions or feelings. Unfortunately, Chris fails to notice that his wife is stressed out and frustrated. She has been having difficulty finding a job and has been cleaning up after both of them.

If she had managed her own emotions more efficiently, she could have brought Chris' attention to the problem and sought a solution. However, it seems that she bottled her emotions until she exploded!

On Chris' end, being more attuned to others' emotions should have tipped him off to the fact that something was bothering his wife: he was too excited to notice how quiet she had been! This situation could have been avoided by both parties.

In the second relationship situation, Andrew is also excited about the new changes in both his job and his location. His husband, however, is having a tough time. Andrew notices his husband's frustration and takes the time to address it. His husband manages his emotions well, and he has a civil conversation with Andrew about his difficulties. They are able to work it out and satisfy both parties.

These examples should show you that Emotional Intelligence in relationships is all about the interaction between two individuals. It is important to be in touch with both your emotions and those of your significant other.

The way that you handle your emotions and respond to those of your partner determines the way that you communicate. For an effective relationship, building and maintaining a high Emotional Intelligence is vitally important!

Emotional Intelligence: Social Interactions

Situation 1

Kelly is a shy person and feels awkward in social groups. She is outgoing only with her own group of friends. One day, her best friend invites her to go out with a group that she is unfamiliar with. Kelly agrees to go. She wants to be more adventurous. Once Kelly and her friend meet up with the group, her friend spends most of her time talking with someone else.

Kelly feels some jealousy but doesn't want it to ruin her night. She listens to the conversation among the other group members and notices that they are all laughing and enjoying themselves. One asks Kelly a question about work, and Kelly perceives her to be genuine and interested. Kelly starts to talk about her job, which helps to relax her. The rest of the night goes smoothly, and Kelly has made some new friends.

Situation 2

Jacob has always been a bit of an outcast. He works from home and has only a couple of friends. He tends to be very sarcastic and insists that people "don't get" his sense of humor. One night his friend is having a viewing party for a football game. Jacob comes along. Some of the guys are annoyed: their team is losing and they've put money on this game.

Jacob doesn't care for football. He feels uncomfortable around new people and cracks some sarcastic jokes at the expense of the losing team. The guys at the party start to dislike him. Jacob's friend is spending more time talking to a girl than to Jacob. Jacob feels more jealous and resentful as the night goes on and nobody talks to him. He leaves early in a frustrated mood.

Analysis

In the first situation, Kelly is shy, which would indicate that she feels some anxiety in new social situations. She recognizes that emotion but doesn't allow it to stop her, and agrees to go out with her friend. When Kelly feels jealous that her friend is not spending time with her, she solves the problem by listening and responding to the other individuals in the group.

She finds that by responding to their cues, she can carry a conversation and even make some new friends! Kelly is showing good control over her emotions. Her responses to her situation are indicative of a high Emotional Intelligence.

In the second situation, Jacob is also uncomfortable in new social situations. Unlike Kelly, he doesn't take the time to accurately read the people around him. If he had, he would have noticed that the guys watching the football game were upset, and maybe he would not have made jokes about their team.

The people watching the game were probably annoyed by Jacob and his jokes, and as Jacob became jealous of his friend, he became less pleasant to interact with. As a result, Jacob ends the evening frustrated.

Further along in the book, we will discuss strategies for navigating social situations similar to the examples given. It isn't always easy to read a room or to say the "right" thing, but we will give you foolproof, step-by-step instructions to get you started.

Emotional Intelligence: Dealing With Fear

Situation 1

Thomas has been having trouble with anxiety for several years. It began with social anxiety in high school and progressed until 30-year-old Thomas is almost completely housebound. New experiences worry him, and he is terrified of straying from his normal routine. He recognizes that his fear is irrational, and wants to change his life.

He wants to try to go to therapy but is scared of such a new experience. He decides to change slowly, every day. He adds something new to his routine each day as he builds his courage. At first, the changes are small; he will have something different for breakfast.

Eventually, he is brave enough to contact an online therapist. After several online sessions, Thomas is ready for referral to a therapist in-person. He is on the road to changing his life.

Situation 2

Lena is a teenager, and at the end of the school year, her

friends are all going to an amusement park. Lena has always enjoyed spending time with her friends, but she has never been on a roller-coaster. She is scared. She gets more and more apprehensive as they approach the park, but she is terrified to mention her fear.

When they reach the park, her friends go straight to the biggest, fastest roller coaster there! Lena stands in line with them, too worried to tell her friends that she isn't sure about going on the ride. Her heart is pounding. She thinks she might faint. She thinks she might cry.

As she and her friends strap into the ride, she starts to cry uncontrollably and shrieks that she wants to get off. It's too late. The ride is already moving, and as it climbs the first hill, she can't stop crying. In 120 seconds, the ride is over, and she is laughing and smiling. It was fun!

Analysis

The first situation deals with an extreme case of fear. There are many individuals who develop minor anxiety and allow it to worsen until their situation is unbearable. Thomas showed a low Emotional Intelligence when he first let his anxiety get out of control. He mistakenly limited everything in his life, hoping it would solve his anxiety, but instead, he trapped himself in a routine.

Luckily, Thomas did develop a high enough Emotional Intelligence to recognize how irrational his behavior was. He took steps to alleviate his anxiety, and ultimately trained himself to work through his fear. He then sought professional help and continued to implement strategies to build his Emotional Intelligence, manage his fear, and continue on to a better life.

The second situation shows an individual who allows their fear to get out of hand and take over. Lena had many opportunities to identify her fear and communicate it to her friends. Her friends could have then helped her to work through her fear, either by convincing her the roller coaster was worth the anxiety, or by helping her to start with a smaller, more manageable ride.

When she didn't express herself, Lena found herself on the most terrifying ride in the park! She allowed herself to be swept along, and because she did not address her fear, it only got worse. When she irrationally explodes and screams to be let off the ride, her anxiety has reached its peak. It is lucky for Lena that it was too late to leave the ride because she almost deprived herself of a very enjoyable experience!

These situations have highlighted just some of the major ways that Emotional Intelligence appears in our daily lives. Now that you have read some examples and seen Emotional Intelligence in action, consider the ways that Emotional Intelligence guides your life. As we've seen here, Emotional Intelligence is not always black and white.

There are some who make decisions based on a poor Emotional Intelligence, but work and build until they are acting with a stronger Emotional Intelligence. We have seen individuals who show Emotional Intelligence traits and individuals who cultivate Emotional Intelligence abilities.

In the next few chapters, we'll present step-by-step guides for recognizing your own Emotional Intelligence traits and building your own Emotional Intelligence abilities.

4 - Uncovering Negative Emotional Patterns

The first step in building your Emotional Intelligence is to identify the negative emotional patterns in your own life. You have seen how personality traits and situations affect our Emotional Intelligence and the ways in which we handle emotional situations. Now you need to consider the "don'ts" of Emotional Intelligence.

These are patterns that we want to eliminate from your life! Building Emotional Intelligence is about identifying and eliminating negative emotional patterns while simultaneously discovering and building positive emotional patterns.

By actively participating in this process, you will gradually learn to replace negative emotional patterns with positive ones. As you learn to assess and manage various emotional situations, you will build your Emotional Intelligence and journey on to lifelong success.

Common Negative Emotional Patterns

These are some generalized negative emotional patterns that seem to fall evenly across the human spectrum. These patterns are easy to adopt and difficult to lose. As you identify these patterns in your own life, try to consider why these patterns have evolved for you.

Avoiding negative feelings

One of the most common mistakes made by individuals who struggle with their Emotional Intelligence is to avoid recognizing negative feelings and emotions. This can lead to "bottling up" feelings and passive aggression and "explosions" later on. Yes, building your Emotional Intelligence is, in part, about trying to maintain a positive state of being.

However, this is not possible if you do not recognize the negative feelings that you have in certain situations and address them immediately. There is NO SHAME in experiencing emotion: even negative emotion! But you do need to recognize that emotion, address the source of that emotion, and decide on a solution to alleviating that emotion.

Spending time with those who maintain negative emotional patterns

There is nothing to be gained by surrounding yourself with individuals who actively seek or passively submit to negative emotional patterns. Peer pressure never ends, even in the adult world! Even if your friends or social group do not actively "pressure" you to behave with negative patterns, it is easy to emulate the people you spend your time with.

We are social creatures, and we adapt quickly to social situations. This means that we try to make ourselves as similar to our peers as possible: we may not even realize that we are doing so. Individuals who are not supportive of your quest to build a stronger Emotional Intelligence will only bring you down. They will encourage negative patterns in your life and make your journey that much more difficult.

Spending time on activities that trigger negative patterns

We all have to take out the trash at some point. Unless you're lucky enough to be able to maintain weekly house-cleaning help, you probably have to clean your house. We have to bring home a paycheck, we have to pay bills. These situations are unavoidable "necessities" to maintaining a life in today's society.

However, there are many areas of our lives that we have control over, even if we feel like we do not. Believe it or not, it is not necessary to pursue a career that you hate. If your job is causing you to fall into negative patterns, again and again, stop and assess.

Do you need to adjust your attitude about your position? Is there joy to be found in the position? If not, then you may need to consider moving on. Examine the activities in your daily life that bring you joy, and spend more time on those while you build your coping skills.

Negative self-talk

Putting yourself down is a common, destructive behavior that leads to negative emotional patterns. There is nothing to be gained by engaging in thoughts and feelings of worthlessness. Individuals with a high Emotional Intelligence are often associated with feelings of confidence. Building confidence can help you to build your Emotional Intelligence. Negative self-talk directly inhibits your progress.

Health Habits That Trigger Negative Emotional Patterns

Your health is important. Building a higher Emotional Intelligence can help you improve your overall health. In the same way, building a healthier body can help you achieve a higher Emotional Intelligence. It is important that you identify your health habits and how they may be affecting you and triggering negative emotional patterns in your daily life.

Avoiding Exercise

All of the medical, psychological, and social advice tells us that we MUST exercise. There is no denying the research that shows that regular exercise makes our lives better. Avoiding exercise is an avoidance behavior that leads to negative emotional patterns.

The less you exercise, the less healthy you are. Your entire body is a precious organism, and keeping the entire organism in optimal health is vital for mental health. Find a type of exercise you enjoy, and pursue it.

Regularly consuming unhealthy foods

Just as keeping your body healthy through exercise benefits your mental health, so does eating right. Consuming unhealthy foods worsens your health every time you eat. You build fat, bad cholesterol, and dehydrate your body. New research is showing that the delicate balance of your gut may play a critical role in your physiological and psychological health.

Consuming processed, artificial, sodium- and sugar-laden foods is a recipe for disaster for your gut. Eating bad simply makes you feel bad. Give your chances a boost by giving your body the fuel that it needs.

Regularly consuming alcohol or recreational drugs

You cannot, cannot maintain a healthy psychological and emotional state of being if there are chemicals in your system with the power to manipulate your thinking or your mood. Alcohol, for example, is a depressant, or a drug that suppresses your immune system and opens the door for negative emotional patterns.

Additionally, addiction is a very serious problem. Those who struggle with their Emotional Intelligence are more prone to addiction and should avoid any addictive drugs, especially while trying to analyze and address their own emotional patterns.

Encouraging addictive behaviors

Addiction is the word we use for becoming dependent on something. Clinically, addiction refers to a drug or a food: some kind of chemical that we put into our body that ignites reward pathways in the brain. Recent research shows that these same reward pathways are lit up by many different stimuli, ranging from sugar to sex.

If there is something in your life that you use as a crutch to get through the day, and you feel you can't live without it, you are encouraging addictive behaviors. Addictive behaviors are a part of a negative emotional pattern that evolves from being unable to face our own negative emotions.

We seek external stimuli to smooth over our negative feelings, and because those negative feelings were never properly addressed, they never truly go away. We continue using external stimuli to smooth over the issue because it is easy, but we fall into the trap of addiction.

Destructive Behavior and Thoughts

A big contributor to negative emotional patterns is destructive thoughts and behavior. Shame, anger, fear, and guilt are all deep thoughts that are difficult to suppress. They are not simple, situational emotions, and they contribute to our patterns of negative emotions.

Additionally, negative emotional patterns can feed into these destructive thoughts and lead to destructive behaviors. Try to identify some of the struggles you have had with these feelings, and examine what patterns and behaviors have contributed to them.

"It's not me it's you": Blaming others

It is easy to blame others for our own negative emotional patterns. Back in Chapter 3, we saw an example of a wife who ended up blaming her husband for the way that she was feeling. He hadn't properly noticed and interpreted her feelings. Rather than recognizing her role in the situation, she lashed out at him over the problem. It is difficult to identify our own faults.

It is a painful process. But as you look over your feelings and actions, remember that you are taking these steps to achieve future success. You are doing something wonderful for your own long-term health!

Recognizing your role in your negative emotional patterns does not mean shifting blame to yourself and encouraging regret. You are simply identifying what actions contributed to the problem. You do not need to atone for these actions in any way: only try to find a solution so these actions do not occur again.

Dwelling on regret

Every human on the planet has made mistakes. If you are a person who is deeply empathetic or has made a mistake that you cannot fix, it often leads to destructive patterns of regret. Managing guilt is a difficult and arduous process.

The simple answer is to try to let go of the past: it is impossible to change it now, and you are on your way to better things! Often, getting rid of guilt and regret is not that simple. Try to identify the patterns of guilt and regret in your own life, and we will discuss solutions to this problem later in the book.

Encouraging fear through avoidance

Avoidance behaviors are often the result of psychological fear. You may feel anxiety about specific situations, or fear of feeling a certain emotion. The fact is, you cannot avoid your fear forever, and your life is not made better by doing so.

Do you remember the example in Chapter 3 that covered the man who allowed his life to be ruled by his anxiety? If you identify exactly what it is you are afraid of, you can begin to set goals and steps to manage and even eliminate that fear. Remember, everyone feels fear. How you respond to that fear is what will rule your life.

Regularly giving in to anger

Anger is possibly one of the most intense emotions. It can rise on a situational basis, or it can simmer for months or even years at a time. Anger is often intertwined with other negative emotional patterns: blaming others, addiction behaviors, avoidance behaviors, or even avoiding exercise.

Just like fear and guilt, anger can rule your life if you allow it to. Giving into anger is never acceptable, and in the long run, it is unhealthy for you. You must evaluate what is causing your anger, your role in that anger, and find ways to address your anger. We will discuss strategies for anger management later in the book.

Seeking retribution

Retribution-seeking is a destructive behavior that is closely related to anger and blaming behaviors. It is important to understand that seeking retribution is not an effective or acceptable way to ease negative feelings regarding an event or situation. Seeking retribution launches a negative pattern that allows you to justify acting in anger and blaming others for the way that you feel.

Perpetuating feelings of shame

Shame is feeling that you have done something inherently wrong that leads to humiliation, anxiety, and guilt. Shame in adult life is often brought on by feeling that society cannot accept you for who you are. Shame is closely intertwined with guilt and maintaining negative social relationships.

To alleviate shame, you must identify what causes you to feel ashamed. Have you done something wrong? Then see the section on guilt and remember, you cannot change the past. Are you surrounded by individuals who cannot accept you or refuse to forgive you? Then it is time to foster relationships with individuals who can love and accept you for who you are.

Identify Negative Patterns and Move Forward

This chapter helped you to identify some common behaviors that can lead to negative emotional patterns. Before beginning the next chapter, take some time to reflect on your own life. What behaviors have you engaged in that are perpetuating negative patterns? What role are you playing in your own negativity? Remember, you cannot solve a problem without first identifying the problem.

Chapter 5 will help you to identify positive behaviors that lead to positive emotional patterns. Many of these behaviors are directly opposite the negative behaviors presented in this chapter. You have identified the problem: now, let's identify what you do well.

5 - Discovering Positive Emotional Patterns

In Chapter 4, you saw a list of negative behaviors and the ways that these behaviors lead to negative emotional patterns. In this chapter, you will read about positive behaviors that lead to positive emotional patterns. Many of these positive behaviors are directly opposite the negative behaviors we discussed in Chapter 4.

As you find behaviors that you use in your own life and those that you do not consider replacing many of the negative behaviors mentioned in Chapter 4 with these positive behaviors. It will be difficult and doesn't happen overnight, but these two chapters are intended to present you with a contrast. These are the behaviors you want to encourage in your daily life.

Common Positive Emotional Patterns

These are some common positive emotional patterns that are seen in individuals that have a high Emotional Intelligence. These patterns encourage positive thinking and are indicative of good strategies for managing your emotions. Consider which of these positive emotional patterns already exist in your daily life, and which of these patterns contrast the negative emotional patterns that may exist in your life.

Acknowledging all feelings and emotions

It is important to acknowledge your emotions as you feel them. There is no such thing as a "bad" emotion: only negative patterns that stem from the ways in which you manage your emotions. Building positive emotional patterns starts with acknowledging your emotions. You should never suppress your feelings. It is okay to feel.

By acknowledging what and how you are feeling, you can then begin to process why you are feeling that way. Acknowledging your feelings enables you to begin examining your emotions objectively, so that you may start brainstorming solutions to negative patterns.

Individuals who possess a high Emotional Intelligence are often characterized by their ability to identify the emotions that they are feeling. Identifying and acknowledging your feelings is the first step to managing your emotions and an important part of building your Emotional Intelligence.

Surrounding yourself with supportive individuals

Having a support system is vital in any endeavor. The presence of a support system is so important, it is often considered a determining factor in whether a terminal patient will live or die, or whether a transplant patient thrives or deteriorates.

Supportive individuals can make or break relationships, careers, and huge life decisions. The common saying "it takes a village" is not only applicable to child-rearing! Spending time with individuals who love and support you will make all the difference as you strive to change your life.

Spending extra time on activities you enjoy

Taking the time to work on enjoyable activities has multiple benefits, from boosting feelings of wellness to boosting your overall self-esteem. Researchers have found that projects and sports are especially beneficial, as they give the participant the feeling that they have accomplished something.

It is important to take time for yourself and cultivate your own interests. In doing so, you build your self-awareness, an important part of Emotional Intelligence.

Learning to Love Yourself

Emotional Intelligence is all about knowing yourself, being able to recognize your emotions and accept them, and looking at your life with a constructive view. In order to achieve this, you must learn to love yourself. If you can love yourself, accepting all of your flaws, you can build confidence.

Confidence is the key to achieving a high self-esteem and ending anxiety in all spheres of your life. The following behavioral patterns will help you determine a pathway to developing a long-lasting relationship with yourself.

Being honest with yourself and with others

Research shows that holding on to secrets and lies can increase anxiety and deteriorate interpersonal relationships. "Being honest" doesn't mean that you have to share every mean thought or every dirty pleasure. Being honest with yourself is very similar to acknowledging your feelings. You are identifying yourself as a person, and acknowledging what makes you, you.

This is an important step in learning to love yourself, which is a huge step in ending fear and anxiety and building Emotional Intelligence. Being honest with others means that you cannot misrepresent yourself. Healthy social interaction does not thrive on lies.

Misrepresenting yourself or lying about your background and opinions can significantly increase your anxiety and self-doubt. In order to surround yourself with positive individuals, you must strive to be open and honest.

Positive self-talk

A second step in building your confidence and love for yourself is positive self-talk. Take the time each day to recognize the things that you have done well. Notice your small and large achievements and take the time to acknowledge and celebrate them.

Do not lie to yourself: simply accept and acknowledge the things that you have done well. Replacing negative self-talk with positive self-talk is a major life change with lifetime benefits.

Constructive Behaviors for Building Positive Emotion Patterns

Building constructive behaviors, or behaviors that serve a purpose in helping you to reach your goals, is another essential piece in building a high Emotional Intelligence. Those with a high Emotional Intelligence are able to act on their emotions after assessing them and come up with solutions to their emotional problems. Fostering constructive behaviors can aid you in this process.

Celebrating others' worth

Often, interpersonal communication problems arise because of deep-rooted jealousy issues harbored by those with a low self-esteem. Taking the time to acknowledge and celebrate the traits in others that you admire is a behavior that can help you to end jealous behaviors and celebrate your relationships with other people.

Remind yourself that others are people just like you: you only see what they want you to see, and many of them may be struggling with similar emotional problems that you are dealing with. Appreciating each individual for who they are will strengthen your interpersonal relationships and build your own self-esteem.

Actively bringing positivity into your train of thought

Building your Emotional Intelligence is all about changing the way that you think. You can actively encourage this process every day by paying attention to the thoughts that you engage in during the day.

Make a special point of noticing when negative thoughts cross your mind. When you are feeling negative about a situation, take the time to acknowledge that feeling and then bring a positive feeling into your train of thought.

For example, if you are thinking "It's such a gloomy day: I can't stand to go to work," then tell yourself that when you get home tonight, you can curl up with a fluffy blanket and a cup of tea. "Seeing the bright side" is an active process, and it will take some effort before it becomes natural.

Practicing forgiveness in your life

In Chapter 4, we discussed feelings of guilt and destructive behaviors like seeking retribution. Studies show that those who intentionally forgive others for wrongdoing are healthier, more positive individuals.

By forgiving others and moving on from situations that have caused you anxiety, anger, stress, or pain, you erase negative patterns from your life and encourage positive behaviors. It is important to actively, mentally forgive an individual, and deliberately put the situation behind you. You will reap psychological benefits from this difficult act.

Acknowledging your fears and facing them

As we discussed in Chapter 4, avoiding your fears gives you no opportunity to overcome them. To encourage positive emotional patterns, you must time the time to acknowledge your fears and find ways to face them.

This does not mean that if you are afraid of heights, you must go skydiving, but rather that if you are afraid of heights and it is interfering in your life, take heights in small, manageable doses until you can build up the courage to handle larger situations.

Perseverance

Above all, you must persevere in your behavioral changes.

Find little ways each day to acknowledge a negative emotional pattern in your life and replace the negative behavior with a positive one. There will be times that you are discouraged. Perhaps you chose to face a fear and it didn't work out: now you are more terrified than before! Setbacks happen.

You must be willing to understand that nothing works out right away! You will feel pushed back or even knocked down at times. It is okay to feel frustrated and angry. What is important is that you always maintain the will to try again.

Replace Negative Patterns With Positive Patterns

Now that you have an understanding of negative patterns and positive patterns, you can begin to identify these patterns in your life. As you move forward, take the time each day, possibly just before bed, to reflect on your day.

Think about the emotional situations that were presented to you throughout the day and how you responded to them. Try to identify the negative patterns and positive patterns that you see. As a guideline, consider the following questions:

- What negative emotional patterns or behaviors did you engage in today?

- How did these patterns affect your handling of emotional situations?

- How did these patterns affect your interpersonal relationships?

- What positive emotional patterns or behaviors did you engage in today?

- How did these patterns affect your handling of emotional situations?

- How did these patterns affect your interpersonal relationships?

- Did you replace any negative patterns with positive ones?

- What patterns are being repeated each day?

By considering these questions, you can assess your abilities in handling your emotions and keep a record of your progress. Remember, big changes start with small steps! No achievement is too small.

By finishing Chapter 4 and Chapter 5, you have learned to identify behaviors that contribute to your Emotional Intelligence. You are learning to replace negative patterns with positive ones. As you continue into the rest of the book, you will learn specific strategies for fostering positive emotional patterns, a vital step in improving your Emotional Intelligence.

6 - Strategies for Improving Your Emotional Intelligence

Now that you have learned what Emotional Intelligence is, how to identify its uses in your life, and how different emotional patterns contribute to your Emotional Intelligence, let's discuss daily activities that you can implement in your life to begin the process of improving your Emotional Intelligence.

First, we will discuss trademark "goals" set by researchers for those who are trying to improve their Emotional Intelligence. Then we will acknowledge conventional advice for lifestyle changes. Finally, you will learn situation-specific activities to help you navigate a social and emotional world.

Skills of a High Emotional Intelligence

When learning a new subject or pursuing a new goal, there are always specific goals that you set out to achieve. This book has focused on "Improving your Emotional Intelligence" and "Eliminating fear," but what specific skills should you seek to achieve in order to reach these lofty goals?

Researchers have targeted this exact question and come up with some basic pillars of Emotional Intelligence that we will strive to build:

Self-Understanding and Awareness

- Recognizing emotions within yourself and identifying them accurately

- Recognizing your own strengths and weaknesses

- Building a strong self-esteem

- Accurately analyze your self-perception

Social Understanding and Navigation

- Building respect for others

- Fostering empathy for others

- Keeping your situation in perspective

Decision-making skills

- Identifying problems and assessing them objectively

- Critical thinking and problem solving

- Taking pride in ethical choices

- Self-reflection

Effective behavior management

- Managing stress and anxiety effectively

- Controlling impulses

- Fostering self-motivation

- Setting goals and enacting plans to achieve them

- Actively engaging in positive behaviors

Building Relationships

- Using clear and effective communication

- Learning to negotiate and cooperate with peers

- Encouraging others

These criteria for improving and measuring Emotional Intelligence are used by researchers across the country in building Emotional Intelligence in children and in adults. Take the time to study them and decide which of these criteria already apply to you, and which you need to work on. Keep these pillars in mind as we discuss strategies for improving your Emotional Intelligence.

Strategies for Building Self-Awareness

Building Self-Awareness is closely related to building your self-esteem and love for yourself. As you learn to respect and love yourself, it will be easier to analyze your emotions and your flaws and to develop strategies for managing them.

Keep a Journal

Monitoring your thoughts, emotions, and progress through writing is an effective way to self-analyze and begin managing your emotions. Journaling, whether on paper or computer, is an effective way to get your thoughts out in front of you so that you can perceive them in a different light.

Research shows that those that consistently journal often have a higher Emotional Intelligence than those that do not. Journaling can be used to let off steam, to acknowledge a feeling that you are having, or to reflect on your day.

Reading past journal entries will help you to monitor your

progress on this journey. Consider starting a new journal to mark the beginning of your life change. You should:

Buy a new journal:

Seek a journal that encourages positive thinking. If bright colors give you a boost, look for a brightly-colored journal. If you enjoy posting an anonymous blog, start up a Tumblr or WordPress account.

Set aside a special time for journaling

This could be at breakfast, during your break at work, or even just before you go to bed. Pair journaling with something you look forward to (like a cup of tea before bed) so that you look forward to journaling each day.

Journal even if you don't feel like it

Journaling can have a way of turning your day around. Encouraging positive emotional patterns begins with taking tiny steps.

Engage in meditation.

Researchers have repeatedly shown that meditation is extremely beneficial to those who practice it regularly. Many people are unfamiliar with meditation and balk at this strange concept. Meditation does not mean that you have to sit cross-legged and chant for hours (though you certainly can if you want to). Meditation simply means taking time out of your day to do nothing else other than reflect. You should:

Eliminate Distractions

Meditation is about allowing your mind to wander freely. You cannot effectively meditate with the television blaring in the background.

Play Non-distracting Music

Soft, instrumental music can boost your brain activity and help the meditation process.

Take Deep Breaths

Breathe in deeply through your nose and out through your mouth. You can be laying down, sitting straight, or even standing with your arms at your sides.

Let it go

Let everything go while you meditate. This is not a time to

worry. It is simply a quiet time to allow your brain to relax. As with journaling, you should strive to make meditation a part of your routine. Choose a specific time of the day to meditate, and make it a priority.

Strategies for Managing Anxiety and Stress

Many individuals who are seeking to boost their Emotional Intelligence are dealing with significant anxiety and stress problems. Anxiety and stress are pervasive emotions that can grow if unchecked. To improve your Emotional Intelligence and build an awareness of these problems, these strategies may be helpful.

Make a plan to manage stress.

If you know that a stressful time is approaching, get organized. Write down important dates and deadlines and partition your work accordingly. Time management is a big part of stress management. Make a plan and stick to it! If this is new for you, try these steps:

Buy a planner with both monthly and weekly calendars. Visualizing your schedule can be an effective way to manage your stress.

Write down all deadlines and important dates in the planner. Use the monthly calendar to identify important dates.

Calculate your time effectively. How long do you have before your deadline? What do you need to complete before then?

Deliberately plan time for each day to get work done. Schedule this time in your planner! If you are a morning person, try to make time in the morning to get important work done. If you know you are exhausted after work, don't try to plan time right after work to complete your tasks! It will not get done.

Plan Rest Time

It is impossible to constantly work every hour of every day. Your brain needs time to recharge, and you need time to relax and reflect. Set aside time every day to keep for yourself. Practice releasing your stress during this time. You can journal, meditate, do yoga, or participate in another activity that calms and focuses you.

Battle Anxiety With Action

When you are feeling anxious, your brain is feeling that

something is wrong: an action must be taken. This often leads to negative behavioral patterns as you limit your activities to alleviate anxiety, or participate in senseless activities to calm yourself. Follow these steps to use positive, constructive action to battle your anxiety:

Identify the things that make you anxious

Are you worrying about an upcoming deadline? Perhaps there is something you can do now to contribute to your work for that deadline. If not, your anxiety may be irrational. Read on.

Find constructive activities that give you joy

Are you crafty, or a handyman? Do you have a pet that needs to be walked? When you start feeling anxious, actively engage in an activity that helps you to feel fulfilled.

Take away one piece of stress

Are you feeling generally anxious but know that you are stressed about the dishes in the sink? Take a few minutes to get them done. Taking away that one stressful factor may help to alleviate your anxiety.

Talk it out. Or you can write.

Talk to a close friend or relative about the way that you are feeling. Write about the way that you are feeling. Getting the problem in front of you can help you to analyze patterns and seek a solution.

Overwhelmed? Make one small change at a time

This book is full of steps and advice. It is easy to feel even more stressed and anxious when presented with lists and lists of steps and behavioral changes that you need to make. You may feel that you have no idea where to begin.

Find one thing—just one—that you know you can implement today. Once you have mastered that change, try another. This is a great way to gradually build confidence and maintain a long-term psychological change. Here are some ideas:

Commit to five minutes of self-reflection each day

Set a timer, and reflect, by journaling, meditating, taking a walk, or doing yoga. Five minutes is shorter than the average shower—you can reflect under the flow of hot water!

Add one healthy food to your diet

If you are struggling with what you eat, this is a great first step for change. Have an apple in the afternoon, or a side salad with your lunch or dinner.

Set your alarm for ten minutes earlier

Adding an extra ten minutes to your morning routine can give you room to "stretch" in the morning. If you typically feel that you are rushing to work, this extra ten minutes can give you valuable breathing room.

Strategies for Building Relationships

Emotional Intelligence isn't only about self-reflection and management. It is also about learning to read and respond to the individuals around you. You may be an individual who is flustered in social situations, or you may be having a hard time connecting to your significant other or to your children. The following are some general guidelines for building strong relationships with others.

Engage in active listening

When a person is talking to you, make a point of hearing them. Acknowledge that you aren't always going to be interested in what they have to say, but recognize that what they are saying is important to them. To build a relationship, you need to make it important to you too.

Stop what you are doing

Try not to fidget or engage in other activities, like watching television, while someone is talking to you. Rote memory tasks like washing dishes or driving usually afford your mind enough space to listen effectively.

Try to make eye contact

If you are driving, this is a bad idea. But if you are at dinner or at work or attending a get-together, making eye contact can help keep you focused on the person who is speaking, preventing your mind from wandering.

Truly consider what the person is saying

Remain objective. A good way to do this is to mentally repeat the words that you hear and come up with questions to further clarify the speaker's intent.

Communicate clearly and honestly

When responding to another person, practice being honest without being offensive. Plainly state what you are thinking, and do not pretend to know facts or have opinions that you do not.

Do

Ask questions

After assessing the topic the speaker is discussing, ask questions to help you with clarification and furthering the conversation. Avoid yes/no questions. Some examples include:

- "How did you get into the business?"

- "I'd like to know more about this subject. Can you point me to some resources?"

- "How long have you been feeling this way?"

Remain honest

If you have no previous experience with a subject, say so, and follow up with a question. This shows that you are interested in learning more.

Remain patient

Conversations are about cooperation between two or more people. You may feel a burning need to say something, but take the time to listen. This will help you effectively "read the room" and respond appropriately to others. Wait before speaking.

Remain open to learning

Don't

Interrupt

Never, ever interrupt, unless you desperately need to leave or are about to have a serious bathroom emergency. Interruption is rude and disrespectful.

Use offensive language

Fostering relationships is about building a bridge. Using offensive language or blatantly stating controversial opinions can burn that bridge quickly.

Ask yes/no questions

These questions limit responses to one word, and one-word conversations get dull quickly.

Spend time and effort on others

Doing things for the people in your life is a wonderful way to show affection, commitment to the relationship, and respect for other individuals. If your wife is exhausted after dinner, take the time to do the dishes, and maybe go the extra mile to make her a cup of tea.

Make plans to do little things for other people. Treat your best friend to coffee, or buy your new coworker breakfast to welcome them to the team. Bringing a little joy to someone else's life will almost always bring joy to yours. Just remember that kindness is only kindness with no strings attached: do not expect repayment or overwhelming gratitude. Simply do.

Consider the feelings of others

Recognizing that others feel and think in similar ways to

you is a major step in building cooperative relationships. Developing empathy is vital to maintaining your relationships. Here are some guidelines to help you navigate your relationships with others:

Make a note of the little things

Is your husband quieter than usual? Does your coworker seem sad on Thursdays? Has your boss been taking a lot of sick leave?

Watch facial expressions

When communicating with others, make a point of looking them in the face (preferably making eye contact). Pay attention to their expressions when they are happy, sad, or angry. With time, you will begin to read facial expressions before any spoken communication, and be able to respond appropriately.

Put yourself in their shoes

Did your coworker work a double today? They are probably tired. Is your girlfriend having trouble coming up with rent? She is probably stressed.

Pay attention to patterns

If your significant other is always exhausted on Fridays, consider planning something special on Fridays. Even an action as simple as ordering a pizza each Friday can be a fun and rewarding activity.

Building relationships is about perceiving and responding, perceiving and responding. As with anything else, the more you practice, the more skilled you will become at understanding how to recognize emotional cues from others.

Maintaining strong relationships will be easier as you learn to efficiently interpret actions and expressions. Responding appropriately is a major benefit of improving your Emotional Intelligence, and you will watch your relationships flourish!

Implementing Strategies in Your Own Life

Now that you have read about different strategies for building different aspects of your Emotional Intelligence, it is time for you to actively implement them. The strategies presented are applicable to a variety of situations, and though they target certain emotions or circumstances, they will assist in improving your overall Emotional Intelligence.

As you continue to grow and learn, use the resources available to you to build on your experience. If yoga helps you manage and contain your emotions, and you are also seeking social interaction, join a yoga studio! The advice of others who are more practiced in the field will benefit you enormously.

Use the internet to find communities and forums for support if you aren't ready for face-to-face social interaction yet. Even if you are, the internet can be a valuable resource. You can find additional advice to supplement what you have already learned from this book. You must be your own coach once you finish this book and move on.

The next few chapters will specifically target difficult obstacles in developing your Emotional Intelligence. Read on to discover how to manage anger and eliminate fear.

7 - Obstacles: Anger and Fear

Fear and anger are some of the most powerful emotions that you will encounter in your life. They often occur in the moment, and can feel insurmountable. When people react strongly in different life situations, they are often motivated by fear, anger, or both. Fear and anger seem to hijack your sense of reason and cause you to act without thinking.

Research has found that emotions like fear and anger are closely linked with our built-in "fight-or-flight" response. When you feel something as strongly as fear or anger, your adrenaline starts moving, and your fight-or-flight response is kicked into high gear. Your body starts pumping more blood and oxygen to your muscles, and the decision-making center of your brain slows down.

This is because fight-or-flight situations call for you to react quickly, without thinking a situation through. This is a good thing if you are being mugged: it is a bad think if you are responding to an everyday life situation. This chapter will focus on calming your fight-or-flight mode on a situational basis as well as provide strategies for dealing with longer-term fear or anger.

Dealing With Situational Anger

Everyone will encounter a situation that makes them angry. Life is frustrating and unfair, and you will encounter other humans who seem determined to make your situation difficult. Before we begin discussing steps for managing your anger on a situational basis, let's discuss some common causes of anger.

What makes you angry?

There are common reasons for everyone to get angry. The following list includes situations or feelings that often lead to intense or even violent anger. If you struggle with anger, consider the following list and think about what often seems to make you angry. Identifying your triggers is a vital step in learning to manage them.

Unfair Situations

It is easy to get angry when you or someone close to you has been treated unfairly.

Feeling Powerless

Unfair situations can often lead to feelings of powerlessness. Being unable to act can cause mental stress and lead to anger.

Responding to Provocation

We often become angry in our interactions with other people or with animals. There are several kinds of provocation that can lead to anger.

Insults

Getting insulted is a type of provocation. We often feel that we must respond to an insult. This behavior is observed by researchers in humans and in animals: we seem to need to defend our honor, or pride, by responding angrily to insults.

Physical Contact

Physical contact is a form of provocation. When another human or animal physically attacks you without invitation, your body can respond by quickly throwing you into fight-or-flight mode.

Increasing Stress

Feelings or stress or frustration that aren't addressed can quickly lead to a flare-up of anger.

Is it ever "okay" to react with anger?

The short answer is no. Anger is an emotion that induces your fight-or-flight response, dampening the processes in the executive decision-making area of your brain. Responding with anger will always mean that you are responding without sufficient thought behind your actions.

Improving your Emotional Intelligence means becoming a person who always considers before acting. Reacting with anger makes this impossible.

Strategies For Managing Your Anger

Recognize your anger

When your anger first flares, you won't be focusing on you, but the object of your anger. Take a moment to realize that you are angry.

Take deep breaths

You are angry. Your body is in 100% fight-or-flight mode. You need to tell your body that this is not a fight-or-flight situation. Breathing slowly and deeply through your nose and out your mouth will slow your heart rate and decrease the flow of adrenaline.

Remove yourself from the situation

If you just can't stay in the room without hitting the guy who just made a rude comment to you, leave. As you learn to manage your anger, you will gradually be able to remain calm while staying in a situation. It is better to leave and calm down than to react.

Take it out somewhere else

When we feel angry, our body feels the need to act. Sometimes calming your heart rate is not enough: your body is ready to go and wants to act. Physical activity is usually most helpful with this. Go to the gym or buy a punching bag.

Engage in "cathartic" activities

Singing loudly to your favorite song blaring through your car stereo, or using art to express your feelings are great ways to get the anger out without getting physical.

Anger That Festers

Sometimes anger is not a quick flare-up that you have to deal with in one situation. Some events can leave you with feelings of anger for months or even years. Someone may have wronged you, you may have fallen on some hard luck, or you may not even have a reason for your anger.

This kind of anger can slowly eat away at your life, making relationships, social interaction, and career success extremely difficult. Your mind focuses and obsesses over your anger, blocking out everything else.

Strategies

Identify negative emotional patterns

Chapter 4 identified some negative emotional and behavioral patterns that result from feelings of anger. Take the time to identify these patterns and try to replace them with positive patterns.

Retribution seeking

This is a negative behavioral pattern. You may feel that you have been wronged and cannot rest until retribution is paid. Research has found that revenge rarely alleviates our frustration, and sometimes can even make our negative feelings worse. Recognize that this is a negative pattern and will only harm you.

Blaming Behaviors

Like retribution-seeking, assigning blame is not productive. You are seeking to manage your anger, and you must recognize your role. You cannot do this if you are intent on blaming others for your situation.

Accept your situation

Blaming others and seeking retribution are not going to change the situation that made you angry. You must accept the situation so that you can take productive steps to improving it.

Get some perspective

When you are constantly feeling angry with your life, it can be helpful to get some perspective. Try volunteering at a soup kitchen or a homeless shelter. Helping others is a great way to make yourself feel better, and a wonderful way to gain some perspective on your life.

Do Not Allow Anger to Rule Your Life!

Anger is a corrosive emotional pattern that must be addressed and rectified. Living your life in anger is not healthy, and research shows that feelings of anger are associated with elevated cortisol levels. Cortisol, also known as the "stress hormone" has well-known negative effects on your health and well being.

Cortisol limits your ability to sleep, to process emotion, and impairs your long-term cognitive ability. If you are struggling with anger, you must take steps immediately to relieve it. If you are planning to implement one small behavioral change at a time to improve your Emotional Intelligence, begin with anger.

Dealing With Fear

Like anger, fear can be situational, or it can be long-term. Long-term fear is usually identified as anxiety or a phobia. Fear can impair every aspect of your life. It can interfere with social interactions, relationships, or your career. Left alone, fear will only grow.

It is a paralyzing monster that can strangle your life! As you identify strategies for managing fear, consider what you are afraid of. Unlike anger, fear does not always fall under a blanket of "common" causes. Fears range from phobias of spiders to a fear of getting intimate with another person. Before you continue reading, reflect on what you are afraid of in your own life. Consider the following questions:

- How does your fear show up in your daily life?

- Are you afraid regularly (more than 1-2 days a week)?

- What causes you to feel afraid?

- Does your fear affect your social life?

- Does your fear affect your relationships?

- Does your fear affect your career?

- Are you hiding from your fear?

The following strategies will help you to manage fear, both situational and long-term, in your daily life.

Strategies for managing situational fear

Take deep breaths

Just like anger, your fear is stimulating your fight-or-flight response. Deep breaths will help to counteract this response and enable you to think clearly.

Assess the situation

Again, there are many reasons to be afraid. The first question you must ask yourself is: Is your life or another's in danger? If not, consider any safety risks to yourself.

Be honest with yourself

What is the worst thing that could plausibly happen in this situation? By "plausibly" we mean that freak accidents (a roller coaster running off the tracks or a plane crashing) are unlikely to occur.

Assess your needs

If your life or another's life is truly in danger, you need to consider all possibilities for removing yourself from the situation. If not, consider whether you need to leave the situation or not. Will the situation benefit you in some way? For example, if you are flying to Paris but are afraid of flying, your "need" is to get to Paris.

Take action

Take every step you need to either remove yourself from the situation or eliminate your fear. If you are on a plane and afraid of flying, use noise-cancellation headphones to block out your surroundings. If you are about to get on a roller coaster and decide you are much too afraid, leave the situation.

Situational fear is tricky and can be frustrating. If you know that you will be in a situation that will engage your fear, plan ahead. Bring noise-cancellation headphones to your flight. Take steps to help yourself.

Strategies For Managing Long-term Fear

Managing long-term fear is similar to managing situational fear. You must identify what you are afraid of. Plan ahead for situations that will cause you fear. Take deep breaths when fear comes on. Assess situations of fear and take to help yourself. For behavioral and emotional strategies for managing fear and anxiety, see Chapter 5.

You can also handle your long-term fear by talking to someone: a friend, family member, even an online forum. Getting your fear out and getting advice from others in similar situations is a great way to start managing fear. Like anger, fear is crippling.

Addressing it is vitally important! All of the steps for improving your Emotional Intelligence will help you to manage your fear as well. Building confidence, interpersonal relationships, and remaining calm are all remedies for fear in your life.

Moving On

Now that you have built an understanding of Emotional Intelligence and its role in your life, as well as addressed specific emotions and ways to manage them, it is time for you to decide what you want and reach for it. Use the strategies provided in this book to boost your confidence and self-awareness.

Do not let fear or anger hold you back! You are in control. You have taken the reins of your life and it is time for you to move on to bigger and better things. You are unstoppable, and it is time for you to blossom!

8 - Conclusion

Thank you again for purchasing this book!

I hope this book was able to help you to build your Emotional Intelligence and take control of your own life.

The next step is to implement positive behavioral changes, find the strategies that work for you and further explore specific methods that apply to your situation. Improving your Emotional Intelligence is an exciting, lifelong journey. You are well on your way. Congratulations on taking this step into self-discovery!

Thank you and good luck!

Thank You

As we reach the end of this book, I want to say thanks for reading this book.

I want to get this information out to as many people as possible. If you found this book helpful, I would greatly appreciate you leaving me a review. This helps others find the book as well.

This book was self-published with the amazing help of Self-Publishing Made Easy Now! [3] . You can grab a free copy of the checklist that started my journey here: FREE Self-Publishing Checklist [4] .

[3] https://selfpublishingmadeeasynow.com/xpjv
[4] https://selfpublishingmadeeasynow.com/free_checklist

Disclaimer

This document is geared towards providing exact and reliable information in regards to the topic and issue covered. The publication is sold on the idea that the publisher is not required to render an accounting, officially permitted, or otherwise, qualified services. If advice is necessary, legal, financial, medical or professional, a practiced individual in the profession should be ordered.

This information is not presented by a financial or medical practitioner and is for entertainment, educational and informational purposes only. The content is not intended as a substitute for professional medical advice, diagnosis, or treatment. Always seek the advice of your physician or other qualified health care provider with any questions you may have regarding a medical condition. Never disregard professional medical advice or delay in seeking it because of something you have read.

The information provided herein is stated to be truthful and consistent, in that any liability, in terms of inattention or otherwise, by any usage or abuse of any policies, processes, or directions contained within is the solitary and utter responsibility of the recipient reader. Under no circumstances will any legal responsibility or blame be held against the publisher for any reparation, damages, or monetary loss due to the information herein, either directly or indirectly.